CHRIST the MASTER TEACHER

CHRIST *the* MASTER TEACHER

THE PURPOSE *and* LESSONS *of* HIS EARTHLY MINISTRY

CORYNNE DAMM

XULON ELITE

Xulon Press Elite
2301 Lucien Way #415
Maitland, FL 32751
407.339.4217
www.xulonpress.com

© 2023 by Corynne Damm

All rights reserved solely by the author. The author guarantees all contents are original and do not infringe upon the legal rights of any other person or work. No part of this book may be reproduced in any form without the permission of the author. The views expressed in this book are not necessarily those of the publisher.

Due to the changing nature of the Internet, if there are any web addresses, links, or URLs included in this manuscript, these may have been altered and may no longer be accessible. The views and opinions shared in this book belong solely to the author and do not necessarily reflect those of the publisher. The publisher, therefore, disclaims responsibility for the views or opinions expressed within the work.

Unless otherwise indicated, Scripture quotations taken from the King James Version (KJV) – *public domain*.

Paperback ISBN-13: 978-1-66286-863-4
Hard Cover ISBN-13: 978-1-66286-864-1
Ebook ISBN-13: 978-1-66286-865-8

Acknowledgments

Thank you to my Savior, Jesus Christ, for saving my soul, giving me the ministry of teaching, and leading me on this path.

Thank you to my parents, Cory and Ruth Damm, for their tireless efforts in rearing, admonishing, and molding me into a servant of God.

Thank you to my brother, Zachary, and his wife, Katelyn, for their constant love and support throughout my life.

Thank you to Pastor Philip Bishop for his godly example, support, and influence in my life.

Thank you to all my teachers for their encouragement, love, and inspiration that have led me to this moment.

Thank you to Dr. Penny Edmonds for her support, encouragement, and advice during this process.

THE PURPOSE of this study is to identify and explore the earthly teaching ministry of Jesus Christ. Five aspects of Christ's earthly ministry were researched and applied to the ministries of modern Christians both in spiritual and secular professions. In chapter I, the people composing the audience of Christ's lessons are identified, and their spiritual, social, and ethnic attributes are examined. In chapter II, the manner of Christ toward those surrounding Him is studied and contrasted with the typical treatment found within their society. In chapter III, the subject matter of Christ's various lessons is compared with the social issues of His day. In chapter IV, the instructional methods observed in the teachings of Christ are equated with modern research-based teaching techniques. Finally, chapter V applies all the previously researched characteristics of Christ's ministry to the modern ministries of every Christian.

Contents

Acknowledgments v
    Chapter I 1
    Chapter II 17
    Chapter III 33
    Chapter IV 51
    Chapter V 67
Bibliography 83
About the Author 87
Endnotes 89

CHAPTER I

WHY DID CHRIST come to earth as a baby, live a perfect life, teach the Scriptures for three years, die a brutal death, and gloriously rise from the dead? Scholars, pastors, and theologians would accurately state that all this was done to finish God's plan of salvation. Many people, however, have marveled about the ministry of Christ as much as, if not more than, His sacrificial death. Even modern secular and Christian teachers follow the principles observed in the teaching methods of the Master Teacher. This split attention should cause others to wonder if dying was the only reason Jesus came to this world over two thousand years ago. Christ was born into the world to save sinners; He accomplished this through His teaching ministry, culminating in the final act of redemption on the cross. While many scholars emphasize the death of Christ, the focus of His earthly ministry was teaching and demonstrating His love through His audience, manner, message, method, and application.

Foremost, Christ was sent to save the whole world; therefore, His audience included individuals from every walk and station in life. John 3:16–17 states, "For God so loved the world, that he gave his only begotten Son, that whosoever believeth in him should not perish, but have everlasting life. For God sent not his Son into the world to condemn the world; but that the world through him might be saved." The emphasis of Christ's earthly ministry was not only to die, as so many scholars surmise, but it was also to teach the lost and dying world about a Savior that loved them and sought to redeem them. His death was the culmination of His earthly purpose and was made possible through His teaching ministry. Luke 2:47–49 records, "And when they saw him, they were amazed: and his mother said unto him, Son, why hast thou thus dealt with us? behold, thy father and I have sought thee sorrowing. And he said unto them, How is it that ye sought me? Wist ye not that I must be about my Father's business?" Even from His earliest recorded dialogues, Christ showed His desire to teach others and fulfill His "Father's business." Homer Kent, Jr. reflects, "Jesus told us why he concentrated his ministry on teaching. He had come as the embodiment of the Word of God, to bring the message of God to men. The absolutely crucial nature of that message explains why Jesus concentrated his ministry upon it."[1] Christ welcomed every willing person to learn from His teachings regardless of His followers' social status, nationality, or morality.

First, every social status was represented in the audience surrounding Christ. Acts 10:34–36 recounts, "Then Peter opened his mouth, and said, Of

Chapter I

a truth I perceive that God is no respecter of persons: But in every nation he that feareth him, and worketh righteousness, is accepted with him. The word which God sent unto the children of Israel, preaching peace by Jesus Christ: (he is Lord of all:)." The social hierarchy of His day held no sway in the ministry of Jesus Christ; therefore, the same love and concern were demonstrated to every person within His ministry. His disciples exemplified His impartiality since they all came from varying backgrounds. Many people followed Christ to hear the words of the Rabbi who accepted all to listen and believe.

Rich members of society sought out the truths and powers manifested in Christ's earthly ministry. Mark 5:22 attests, "And, behold, there cometh one of the rulers of the synagogue, Jairus by name; and when he saw him, he fell at his feet." Jairus sought out Jesus because he had heard of the miracles performed and desired Jesus to heal his daughter. John D. Grassmick notes that Jairus was highly respected within the community and was responsible for the management and worship of the synagogue.[2] Therefore, Jairus asking help from Jesus would be astonishing since Jairus had much sway within the community and would have many resources at his disposal. This leader had expended all his available assets and could turn to no one other than Jesus; thus, the Master answered this desperate man's plea by following him back to his house. There, Jairus and his family were saved after Jesus raised their daughter to life.

Another instance was recorded in the Gospels regarding a young ruler seeking Christ for affirmation of eternal life. Matthew 19:21–22 recalls, "Jesus said unto him, If thou wilt be perfect, go and sell that thou hast, and give to the poor, and thou shalt have treasure in heaven: and come and follow me. But when the young man heard that saying, he went away sorrowful: for he had great possessions." In contrast to the meeting with Jairus, this young man left the presence of Jesus without any record that he ever accepted the salvation offered; this ruler loved his earthly affluence more than the heavenly riches available if he were but to follow the Savior. The example of the young noble proved the need for repentance when seeking out the truth.

A third example of the affluent seeking Christ can be observed in the Gospel of John. John 4:46 records, "So Jesus came again into Cana of Galilee, where he made the water wine. And there was a certain nobleman, whose son was sick at Capernaum." Once again, a man of high standing within the community determined to find the Savior and receive His healing. Believing in the power of Christ, the noble returned home with the faith that his son was healed; as a result, his son was cured physically, and the man's household was saved spiritually through this interaction with Christ. Christ's ministry not only touched the lives of the rich but also extended into the hearts of the needy.

Poor members of society thronged Him to hear about a God who was not "a respecter of persons."

Chapter I

John S. Sewall notes that Christ Himself was a poor man.[3] Several times throughout the Scriptures, Christ is referred to as the "carpenter" or "carpenter's son." Christ also stated in Matthew 8:20 that "foxes have holes, and the birds of the air have nests; but the Son of man hath not where to lay his head." Christ had a great love for those in society who were poor in spirit or wealth. Lester Reddin, in his article "Jesus the Rabbi," notes the distinctive way in which Christ treated those in His audience:

> Noteworthy is the consideration which he had for the individuality of his pupils. He recognized that not all men are cast in the same psychological mold, and therefore he never required any one to be other than himself. He dealt with each one according to his characteristic endowment, his courage or his timidity, his ease or his difficulty in apprehending the truth. He was not willing that any one should fail, from the lack of patient restatement and elucidation, to grasp the great truths which he taught.[4]

The outcasts of society loved and followed Jesus wherever He went because they knew that Christ would accept them and teach them the Scriptures. Christ saw their hearts rather than their outward appearance, and the poor loved Him for His intuition. Jesus was not hampered by the social standings of His time and applauded the sacrifices of the destitute. Mark 12:42–44 recounts the observation of Christ while in the temple:

> And there came a certain poor widow, and she threw in two mites, which make a farthing. And he called unto him his disciples, and saith unto them, Verily I say unto you, That this poor widow hath cast more in, than all they which have cast into the treasury: For all they did cast in of their abundance; but she of her want did cast in all that she had, even all her living.

This poor woman gave her best to God, and even her pitiful amount was worth more than the heaping offerings of the rich because she gave all her wealth. She sacrificed much in her life with the little she offered and was more blessed than the pompous crowds who gave with conceit and self-gratification. Christ was more focused on the hearts of individuals than He had ever been interested in the monetary achievements of people.

Second, every nationality benefited from the earthly teaching ministry of Christ. Matthew 28:19 attests, "Go ye therefore, and teach all nations, baptizing them in the name of the Father, and of the Son, and of the Holy Ghost." The Great Commission, spoken by Christ, exhorts every believer to share the gospel with all peoples, nations, and tongues. While on earth, His primary ministry was directed at His chosen people, Israel, yet He never turned away the seeking Gentile or condemned individuals based on their nationality.

Christ's earthly teachings and miracles primarily focused on the Jews, yet one of the saddest pieces of Scripture reveals how the nation that housed the Savior of the world was also the first to reject Him. John 1:11 states, "He came unto his own, and his own received him not." Many Jews were so blinded by their traditions and earthly cares that they missed the coming of the much-desired Messiah. John 1:12 counters, "But as many as received him, to them gave he power to become the sons of God, even to them that believe on his name." Despite the rejection of many, some still accepted Christ and made Him their Savior; these individuals went on to spread His truths with their neighbors and friends, becoming some of the first missionaries. Edward A. Blum notes that Jesus came first to the nation of Israel.[5] This precedent was not because He loved Israel more than the rest of the world, but Israel was His chosen people and His witness to the surrounding nations. Exodus 19:6 commands, "And ye shall be unto me a kingdom of priests, and an holy nation. These are the words which thou shalt speak unto the children of Israel." From the beginning, God desired the Israelites to be a light to the world. John D. Hannah comments that Israel was chosen to be separate from the nations as an example to the world.[6] Israel was the nation from which the Messiah would be delivered, and each Jew had a responsibility to represent God to the surrounding peoples. Just as the priests were to be holy and physically perfect, the Israelites were to be a "peculiar" people to the Gentiles. While Christ came as a Jew and lived among them, He was not exclusive in His redemption, because Jesus Christ came to save the whole world, not just one people group.

Gentile people were not exempt from the healing and forgiving hand of the Master, for all who sought redemption were accepted. Christ was not a "respecter of persons" and was "not willing that any should perish." Matthew 15:22–28 records:

> And, behold, a woman of Canaan came out of the same coasts, and cried unto him, saying, Have mercy on me, O Lord, thou Son of David; my daughter is grievously vexed with a devil. But he answered her not a word. And his disciples came and besought him, saying, Send her away; for she crieth after us. But he answered and said, I am not sent but unto the lost sheep of the house of Israel. Then came she and worshipped him, saying, Lord, help me. But he answered and said, It is not meet to take the children's bread, and to cast it to dogs. And she said, Truth, Lord: yet the dogs eat of the crumbs which fall from their masters' table. Then Jesus answered and said unto her, O woman, great is thy faith: be it unto thee even as thou wilt. And her daughter was made whole from that very hour.

This woman sought Jesus for her daughter who was afflicted with demons, but Jesus' response differed from what would be expected. Matthew Henry comments that Christ's reply to this woman was not done out of a lack of love for the Gentiles but ensured that she came to Him in humility.[7] Jesus knew this woman's heart, but He still wanted to test her outward response to an insensitive comment. The woman came in humility and demonstrated a key factor in true repentance and redemption. This Gentile woman understood that she needed to humble herself in order to receive the blessing and healing of Christ.

Another instance involved Jesus and a Roman centurion. Matthew 8:13 records, "And Jesus said unto the centurion, Go thy way; and as thou hast believed, so be it done unto thee. And his servant was healed in the selfsame hour." This man demonstrated great faith in Christ's healing power and sought the Master for the restoration of his dying servant; he proved his understanding that Christ had authority over sickness when he likened Jesus to a military commander relaying orders and expecting complete obedience. Jesus applauded this man's faith, healed the servant, and saved the heart of the centurion. This man's awareness of Christ's identity validated his faith in the God of the universe.

However, Gentiles did not perform all the seeking during Christ's earthly ministry. J. Dwight Pentecost records that Christ approached a Gentile with the purpose to minister and save.[8] Jesus determined to go through Samaria to meet the woman at the well. John 4:7 relates, "There cometh a woman of Samaria to draw water: Jesus saith unto her, Give me to drink." Jesus knew this woman was on her way to that exact well at that exact time, and He sought her out. He broke many rules in so doing, as Edwin Blum correlates that a Jewish rabbi would have rather gone thirsty than talk with a strange Samaritan woman.[9] Despite social customs and expectations, Christ sat down and engaged this woman in a spiritual conversation. John 4:10 expounds, "Jesus answered and said unto her, If thou knewest the gift of God, and who it is that saith to thee, Give me to drink; thou wouldest have asked of him, and he would have given thee living water." Jesus found this woman to tell her of the One who could give her spiritual life; He was not concerned about her difference in nationality but focused on her spiritual need. Because of His patience and all-knowing care, an entire city of Gentiles was saved through this woman's testimony. John 4:39–41 recounts, "And many of the Samaritans of that city believed on him for the saying of the woman, which testified, He told me all that ever I did. So when the Samaritans were come unto him, they besought him that he would tarry with them: and he abode there two days. And many more believed because of his own word." Jesus Christ came to save all people who were willing to repent, regardless of their ethnicity.

Third, every lifestyle was represented in the crowd that followed Jesus and listened to His teachings.

Chapter I

Mark 2:16 records, "And when the scribes and Pharisees saw him eat with publicans and sinners, they said unto his disciples, How is it that he eateth and drinketh with publicans and sinners?" Christ was not selective in the audience He taught, nor was He judgmental like the other religious leaders present. Jesus focused on reaching the hearts of people willing to admit their sins and repent of their wrongdoing, while the religious leaders followed Him because they were either intrigued by His message or sought to destroy Him. The sinners listened closely to Him because He offered them healing and forgiveness that they lacked from the others in society.

Self-righteous leaders were amazed by the humility and understanding that was present in Christ's testimony. Luke 2:46 recollects, "And it came to pass, that after three days they found him in the temple, sitting in the midst of the doctors, both hearing them, and asking them questions. And all that heard him were astonished at his understanding and answers." Even as a child, Jesus astounded the religious scholars with His questions and understanding of scriptural prophecies and doctrine. This reaction continued into His earthly ministry as many learned men listened to His doctrine, explanation of the Scriptures, and interpretation of the law. Gary Cate comments that Christ addressed the scribes in His audience with subjects that pertained especially to them.[10] Many of the scribes and Pharisees who listened to the teachings of Christ were jealous and desired to rid themselves of the man who questioned their authority and pointed out their hypocrisy. Mark 12:12–13 records, "And they sought to lay hold on him, but feared the people: for they knew that he had spoken the parable against them: and they left him, and went their way. And they send unto him certain of the Pharisees and of the Herodians, to catch him in his words." Numerous religious leaders allowed their self-righteousness and power lust to blind them from the truth.

While many religious leaders followed simply to condemn Christ, some truly wanted to learn the truths that He taught. John 3:1–2 records, "There was a man of the Pharisees, named Nicodemus, a ruler of the Jews: The same came to Jesus by night, and said unto him, Rabbi, we know that thou art a teacher come from God: for no man can do these miracles that thou doest, except God be with him." Nicodemus, a Pharisee, desired to learn the truths of the Lord; to accomplish this, Nicodemus had a private meeting with Christ. During this meeting, Christ spoke one of the more famous Bible verses, John 3:16. Nicodemus sought the truth and most likely believed in the deity of Christ at this moment or soon after, as he was one of the few who cared for the body of Jesus. While His message was for all who listened, Christ did not come to witness to the righteous, but to the sinners in need of repentance.

Sinful people were humbled that a rabbi would stoop to teach them and demonstrate such compassion. Matthew 9:11–12 states, "And when the Pharisees saw it, they said unto his disciples, Why eateth your Master with publicans and sinners? But when Jesus heard that, he said unto them, They that be whole need not a physician, but they that are sick." Jesus came to redeem sinners and return them into the Father's fold—a job that the religious leaders should have been busy in but had neglected. Mark 6:34 recounts, "And Jesus, when he came out, saw much people, and was moved with compassion toward them, because they were as sheep not having a shepherd: and he began to teach them many things." Jesus Christ observed the spiritual state of Israel and was moved with love and concern for their lost condition.

Many of these sinners followed Christ after He healed them from physical maladies. Luke 8:2 recounts, "And certain women, which had been healed of evil spirits and infirmities, Mary called Magdalene, out of whom went seven devils." Mary Magdalene's life before Christ was a dark time filled with the machinations of demonic beings. John A. Martin notes that the number seven often meant completion; therefore, Mary Magdalene was fully possessed.[11] This woman had been wholly claimed by demons, but Christ freed her from her spiritual bondage; and consequently, she followed Him throughout His earthly ministry and was the first to see Jesus after He rose from the dead. Jesus' inner circle was composed of once openly sinful men and women because Christ did not hesitate being seen with sinners.

Some who were delivered from their demons were compelled to remain in their homeland and witness to their families. Mark 5:15 records, "And they come to Jesus, and see him that was possessed with the devil, and had the legion, sitting, and clothed, and in his right mind: and they were afraid." This demon-possessed man roamed within the tombs of this settlement. John Martin comments that a legion was six thousand soldiers in the Roman army.[12] This Gentile man's life reflected this overtaking with his violence and dwelling place, since he had been driven to live within the tombs and spent his days and nights crying and cutting himself; yet when Christ appeared, the demons were sent into the pigs, and the man's sanity returned. This man of the Gadarenes was sent home to bear witness of the change in his life because of the influence of Christ. Jesus Christ spent His ministry touching the lives of His audience and driving away their infirmities.

Jesus included a variety of backgrounds and beliefs when He called His twelve disciples. Wilmington records two disciples of Jesus who had either a checkered past or future—Matthew and Judas Iscariot.[13] Even though Christ knew of their past deeds and present thoughts, He still called both to follow Him. Matthew Henry marvels at the grace shown through Christ's choosing of Levi, Matthew, as one of His disciples.[14] This grace was shown to a man viewed as a traitor to his nation. John

Chapter I

A. Martin supports this view that Matthew was believed to have betrayed his people for the material gain afforded him through his position with the Romans.[15] Many Jews greatly disliked tax collectors because they were often dishonest and characterized the oppressors of Israel. Despite the negative sentiments toward Matthew, Jesus called him to be one of His twelve disciples. Matthew demonstrated his desire to follow Christ by having a large feast at his home and willingly leaving all his wealth to follow the Savior wherever He went.

In contrast, Judas Iscariot, who eventually betrayed Christ, was also chosen as one of the twelve disciples. Edwin Blum expounds that at the Lord's Supper, the disciples missed Christ's sign of Judas' betrayal and thought only good of him.[16] Judas had deceived everyone but Jesus with his semblance of sincerity. While Matthew had changed in both his lifestyle and his heart, Judas Iscariot masterfully hid his true intentions and remained open to the eventual possession of Satan. Despite knowing the outcome, Jesus Christ still called Judas into His inner circle and extended His trust to him. Like the apostle Paul in I Timothy 1:15 declares, "This is a faithful saying, and worthy of all acceptation, that Christ Jesus came into the world to save sinners; of whom I am chief." Judas Iscariot was one of the sinners that Christ desired to save, and Jesus' redemptive hand stretched to Judas despite his imminent betrayal.

The audience of Christ was as varied and all-inclusive as salvation, for Christ came into the world that He might teach all people about the God who loved them and wanted to have a special relationship with them. Nationality, appearance, social status, and lifestyle had no bearing on the affection of the Master Teacher; He was concerned only with the decisions made regarding salvation. Christ's cry to the world remained the same, as can be seen in Matthew 15:10: "And he called the multitude, and said unto them, Hear, and understand." May all who still hear obey this call, repent of their sins, and turn to follow the One who gave it all.

Chapter II

JUST AS THE identity of His audience differed greatly throughout His ministry, Christ transmitted heavenly truths to the crowds in a distinct and varying manner. As a result of His outstanding conduct in every situation, people flocked to hear all that the young rabbi had to teach them from the Scriptures. John S. Sewall remarks on the behavior of Christ during His time on earth:

> When we look at Jesus himself we note how finely he was adapted to just this work of social renovation. In person and character he was a God. In sympathies he was a man, and understood men. In spiritual gifts he was equipped with a revelation of divine love and divine grace to save men. In miraculous endowment he had power over the forces of nature, exorcised both demons and disease, held the keys of life and death. He claimed that all authority had been committed to him. His life, his character, his teachings, show how competent he was to assume that royal

trust. And his works show him using it—a kingly dispenser of gifts from heaven.[17]

Jesus Christ was fully God while simultaneously being entirely man; this symbiotic identity can be observed in the teachings and life of the Lord. To a world blinded by the darkness of sin, He brought heavenly truths enveloped in earthly comparisons. People flocked to His side and listened raptly to complicated verity made understandable through earthly scenarios. Christ used His authority, love, and godliness to impart necessary lessons to His listeners.

First, He taught the crowds with an authority that demonstrated His deity. Mark 1:22 relays, "And they were astonished at his doctrine: for he taught them as one that had authority, and not as the scribes." Christ communicated in such a way that all who listened to Him could not believe His understanding and confidence. Jesus was not a formally educated man who had studied the Scriptures for years or had the best tutors to lead Him through the intricacies of the Word, yet Christ interpreted the words of old and taught their truths to gaping audiences. Matthew Henry notes that the doctrine presented by Christ was astonishing and admirable to all who heard it.[18] Jesus introduced the people to a life of service, redemption, grace, and victory. The Jews would have been surprised at this because their lives had been so governed by sacrifices and the traditions of their religion that they had forgotten the reasons behind their actions, yet Jesus

Christ wanted to return the fervency and dedication that was once known by His people and establish a new relationship with individuals through the fulfillment of the law. Luke 4:32 comments, "And they were astonished at his doctrine: for his word was with power." His authority, which was granted by God the Father, afforded a special power to all His teachings and actions.

His insightful remarks were not the only aspects that portrayed His authority and deity. John A. Martin mentions how Jesus' miracles provided further proof of His heavenly power.[19] Casting out demons who acknowledged His godhead and healing the sick reinforced the authority of Christ's ministry and provided physical proof of His deity. Though the religious leaders questioned Christ, intending to expose Him as a fraud, Christ demonstrated His authority each time and rebutted their feeble attempts. Matthew 22:29 records, "Jesus answered and said unto them, Ye do err, not knowing the scriptures, nor the power of God." These leaders attempted to confuse the Savior by twisting the Scriptures, but this perversion merely illuminated their own ignorance and misinterpretation of the ways of God. Louis A. Barbieri, Jr. notes that the scribes failed to understand the Word of God, and Christ denounced them for their lack of comprehension.[20] The Lord revealed the faults of these men and taught them the true meaning of the words they misrepresented. The actions and voice of the

Lord commanded the obedience and respect owed to a person of authority.

His mannerisms were not the same as a common man but required absolute attention and awe. Jesus Christ spent His ministry healing the sick, raising the dead, casting out demons, and teaching all who would listen about a God who loved and desired to save His people from their sins. Mark 5:20 records, "And he departed, and began to publish in Decapolis how great things Jesus had done for him: and all men did marvel." When Jesus healed the demoniac of the Gadarenes, the man was charged with circulating how such healing was wrought in his life. Every person who heard of this miracle wondered at it, and many believed because of this man's testimony. Jesus further illustrated His deity when He read the Scriptures in the synagogue. Matthew 13:54 recounts, "And when he was come into his own country, he taught them in their synagogue, insomuch that they were astonished, and said, Whence hath this man this wisdom, and these mighty works?" Even when Christ returned to His hometown of Nazareth, people that He grew up with marveled at His knowledge and interpretation of the Scriptures. They did not accept Him as the Messiah, yet their hearts were stirred by the uncommon comprehension of the carpenter's son.

Christ's righteous indignation also demonstrated His godly authority over every man. Matthew 23:13 exposes the wickedness in the hearts of the religious leaders: "But woe unto you, scribes and

Pharisees, hypocrites! for ye shut up the kingdom of heaven against men: for ye neither go in yourselves, neither suffer ye them that are entering to go in." Jesus had no qualms when pointing out the sinfulness of the self-important and self-righteous religious leaders of that time. The way Christ dealt with the sin of these men differed greatly from His treatment of others because the religious leaders held their self-proclaimed righteousness over the common people. Since these men published their spiritual contributions, Christ overtly listed their flaws and need for repentance.

Christ also demonstrated an uncommon aversion to the religious traditions and compromises of the Jewish culture. John 2:14–16 exhibits Christ's anger regarding the pollution of His Father's house:

> And found in the temple those that sold oxen and sheep and doves, and the changers of money sitting: And when he had made a scourge of small cords, he drove them all out of the temple, and the sheep, and the oxen; and poured out the changers' money, and overthrew the tables; and said unto them that sold doves, Take these things hence; make not my Father's house an house of merchandise.

Uncommon actions revealed an authority known only to God; at this point, Christ showed everyone in the temple that He was the Son of God and had the right to throw out the perversion found within its walls. Charles C. Ryrie notes that Christ dealt with the sin of sacrilege because the people defamed His temple with their moneymaking schemes.[21] The cacophony of the animals and men calling out for the worshipers to buy their goods destroyed the atmosphere needed for true reverence and reflection. Upon viewing the atrocity, Christ braided a cord of ropes and proceeded to deal with the problems of the religious system. J. Dwight Pentecost also observes that Christ's response was a complete demonstration of His authority and righteous anger.[22] Jesus was incensed by the negligence and utter disrespect shown by those within the temple, and His response swiftly ceased such deviations from the Scriptures.

His voice commanded the respect of others and consistently portrayed His feelings for His audience and topic. Luke 4:36 states, "And they were all amazed, and spake among themselves, saying, What a word is this! for with authority and power he commandeth the unclean spirits, and they come out." Just as in the beginning when the world was created, Christ's authority was translated through His words when He sent demons out of tormented people. Not only was His deity represented in His voice, but His love and concern for the spiritual and physical well-being of others were clearly demonstrated.

His care for the people can also be noted through His forgiveness of sin and healing of infirmities. Matthew 9:6 comments, "But that ye may know that the Son of man hath power on earth to forgive sins, (then saith he to the sick of the palsy,) Arise, take up thy bed, and go unto thine house." His voice had such power that every sin of a repentant individual could be forgiven, and their soul could be saved from eternal punishment. Christ was not willing that any person should experience the fires and eternal separation of hell. His aversion to the eternal punishment of mankind was present in His discourse with the people. Gary Cate notes that Christ entreated His audience to search the Scriptures and find the truth for themselves.[23] Jesus desired everyone to believe in Him, and His urgency can be seen throughout His teachings. Christ's powerful instruction exhibited His great love for mankind.

Second, all His teachings and actions were accomplished through an undying love. John 15:9 declares, "As the Father hath loved me, so have I loved you: continue ye in my love." Christ had an everlasting love for the world, and this doctrine contrasted the one being taught by the Pharisees and Sadducees. The people of Christ's time were starved for the affection and compassion that they experienced when they were in the presence of Christ, so much so that Christ extended His care for others past the brevity of His time on the earth. John 15:13 asserts, "Greater love hath no man than this, that a man lay down his life for his friends." Foretelling His own death, Jesus taught the absolute meaning of selfless love; for in this verse, a man is dying for his friends, but the Lord Jesus Christ also died for His enemies. For those in sin, Christ had abundant love and forgiveness; and He disapproved of the machinations of the self-righteous. John 8:7 documents, "So when they continued asking him, he lifted up himself, and said unto them, He that is without sin among you, let him first cast a stone at her." The religious leaders had set a trap for the Lord when they brought a woman caught in adultery, yet Christ was not fooled by their evil designs and refused to fall for their conspiracies. He challenged the accusers to search their own hearts before they cast judgment upon the woman caught in sin. One by one, the religious leaders left until there were only Christ and this woman. Once everyone had departed, Christ asked the woman whether there was no other person present to punish her for her sin. John 8:11 concludes, "She said, No man, Lord. And Jesus said unto her, Neither do I condemn thee: go, and sin no more." While being the only person without sin, Jesus forgave the woman for her transgressions and offered her the redemption she needed for her misdeeds.

His compassion was overwhelming and motivated the subject of His teaching. Matthew 9:36 relays, "But when he saw the multitudes, he was moved with compassion on them, because they fainted, and were scattered abroad, as sheep having no shepherd." Jesus observed the spiritual mood of the people and desired to change their fallen condition. Just as Psalm 23 states that the Lord is the

Chapter II

Good Shepherd, so Jesus looked upon the children of Israel as His lost sheep that required Him to protect and lead. His love was manifested through the compassion directed toward the struggles of His people. Matthew 14:14 records, "And Jesus went forth, and saw a great multitude, and was moved with compassion toward them, and he healed their sick." His compassion extended from the spiritual deficits to the physical frailties of people. Matthew 20:34 continues, "So Jesus had compassion on them, and touched their eyes: and immediately their eyes received sight, and they followed him." Because Jesus was willing to heal the physical maladies of the people, crowds sought His company; and more individuals were exposed to the compassion and salvation offered by Christ. Through His example of love, Christ showed His society that everyone is deserving of care and kindness. Warren Wiersbe expounds on this idea when he notes that Christ taught an unforgiving world to love one another.[24] Society was unwilling to accept the sinful, disabled, and impure; yet Christ openly invited every person to partake of the love He offered. Matthew 18:33 further states, "Shouldest not thou also have had compassion on thy fellowservant, even as I had pity on thee?" Christ desired His audience to realize that they too needed forgiveness, mercy, and compassion, just as their less fortunate neighbors. Jesus taught the crowds to demonstrate a godly love to their fellow man.

His empathy allowed Him to relate with the everyday struggles of His listeners. Hebrews 4:15

expounds, "For we have not an high priest which cannot be touched with the feeling of our infirmities; but was in all points tempted like as we are, yet without sin." Christ came and lived just as a man with all the weaknesses and difficulties that are a part of this sin-cursed world, yet He remained pure and blameless before the Lord and man. Despite His spiritual victory, Christ still subjected Himself to the cruelty and punishment of sin—death. Philippians 2:7–8 further states, "But made himself of no reputation, and took upon him the form of a servant, and was made in the likeness of men: And being found in fashion as a man, he humbled himself, and became obedient unto death, even the death of the cross." Being without sin yet willing to die for sinful man afforded Christ an understanding of His creation that no false deity can offer. Matthew Henry mentions that it was necessary for God to experience the same testing and struggles as His creation.[25] No cult or other religion has a prophet or god who suffered through the trials of human existence, was falsely accused, killed, and conquered the finality of death. This was all accomplished to demonstrate how man can live in holiness by trusting in a God who suffered all. Matthew 8:20 further says, "And Jesus saith unto him, The foxes have holes, and the birds of the air have nests; but the Son of man hath not where to lay his head." Jesus was not born into wealth but poverty, and He spent much of His adult life surviving on the generosity of His followers and friends. Without His companions' hospitality, Christ spent His nights sleeping outside under the stars or in a tent. Jesus Christ exemplified the suffering of humanity to a world dying with a need for love and forgiveness.

Third, His teachings introduced His audience to a godliness unknown to them. Matthew 5:46 presents, "For if ye love them which love you, what reward have ye? do not even the publicans the same?" Jesus challenged the people to love their enemies and show a godly concern for others. The world struggled in demonstrating a care that was so unpopular and uncommon to individuals who sought the hurt of others. Jesus even expanded His teachings when He demonstrated this principle in His own life. This selfless care is evident when some of His last words before His death included His forgiveness of His tormentors. Luke 23:34 relays, "Then said Jesus, Father, forgive them; for they know not what they do. And they parted his raiment, and cast lots." As the world jeered and blasphemed God, the creator of the universe begged forgiveness for the enemies He came to save. His final example was a culmination of the truths He imparted throughout His earthly ministry.

Hard truths from the Scriptures were introduced in an understandable manner. Christ did not waste His time with long speeches and eloquent language but simply imparted the ways of God in a manageable address. Larry D. Pettegrew comments on how Christ differed greatly from the religious leaders because the people could understand the ideas He conveyed:

One could choose any of the passages from Christ's teaching and come up with the same conclusion: Christ's manner of teaching was that of simplicity. Just because Christ's manner of teaching was simple, however, does not mean that the content was shallow. Harrison says: "A certain peril lurks behind this simplicity. It is the danger that the reader of the Gospels may assume, without realizing it, that the truths Jesus enunciated are as easy of comprehension (and execution) as the linguistic medium that conveys them to the ear. His words are simple, yet no words could be more profound. Stripped of all needless accessories, they transmit the truth in all its boldness and severity such as only an unheeding familiarity can obscure." Without a doubt this simple, yet profound, manner of teaching was a main aid in making Christ an interesting teacher.[26]

Jesus taught familiar principles to His audience in a style that stressed the need for inward changes rather than an outward conformance. The Jews were so callous to the law because they were so accustomed to steeling their actions with a sense of obedience and understanding, yet Christ tore down their presumptions and challenged His audience to inspect their motives and innermost thoughts. Christ did not come to destroy the law but to make it meaningful in the lives of His listeners.

Chapter II

The law was compared to the sin present in the heart of man. Matthew 5:17–18 introduces, "Think not that I am come to destroy the law, or the prophets: I am not come to destroy, but to fulfil. For verily I say unto you, Till heaven and earth pass, one jot or one tittle shall in no wise pass from the law, till all be fulfilled." Christ came to complete the law and make it more understandable to His audience. Dr. Harold Willmington notes that Christ amplified the law rather than diminished it.[27] Jesus made the law more applicable to the lives of His audience because He stressed the importance of changing inwardly rather than embellishing their outward responses. Matthew 23:23 challenges, "Woe unto you, scribes and Pharisees, hypocrites! for ye pay tithe of mint and anise and cummin, and have omitted the weightier matters of the law, judgment, mercy, and faith: these ought ye to have done, and not to leave the other undone." The religious leaders, who were supposed to represent the Lord to the people, had slowly removed the heart of God from the teachings of the law. People were judged and discarded for their sin while these leaders harbored an inward delight in criticizing others when their own hearts were corrupt. Matthew 5:21–22 continues Christ's inspection of the internal condition of His people:

> Ye have heard that it was said by them of old time, Thou shalt not kill; and whosoever shall kill shall be in danger of the judgment: But I

say unto you, That whosoever is angry with his brother without a cause shall be in danger of the judgment: and whosoever shall say to his brother, Raca, shall be in danger of the council: but whosoever shall say, Thou fool, shall be in danger of hell fire.

Christ reminded the people of the law and furthered its influence to matters of the heart instead of just outward obedience. The Jews had been consumed by the need for sacrifices and traditions that slowly distracted them from the true meaning of their actions. All these activities were established to show the people how disgusting their sin was and their need for redemption through the sacrifice of perfect blood. Jesus arrived to be the ultimate sacrifice and fulfill the law that had governed the lives of the Jewish people. The law offered no mercy for sinners and portrayed how truly despicable each person was because of their sin, yet Christ introduced a new aspect to the law when He taught the people about the grace of God.

Grace was freely established and offered to all who would listen and believe. Matthew 5:43–44 demonstrates, "Ye have heard that it hath been said, Thou shalt love thy neighbour, and hate thine enemy. But I say unto you, Love your enemies, bless them that curse you, do good to them that hate you, and pray for them which despitefully use you, and persecute you." The Lord taught a confused crowd about the measure of grace needed to cover their sins as well as those of others. Just as God offered grace to every man, each person was expected to extend the same kindness, even to those who hated and desired to destroy him. This point of view created much disturbance in the hearts and minds of the common and religious people of His day. No one had ever shared such forgiveness and understanding with them, and the suggestion of grace was unnatural to all who heard Christ teaching on the subject. Luke 6:32 expounds, "For if ye love them which love you, what thank have ye? for sinners also love those that love them." The principles detailed in these verses were unnatural and convicting for the crowds gathered to hear the teachings of Christ. Jesus demonstrated the grace He taught when He dealt with the myriad of people with whom He came into contact, and He desired His followers to demonstrate this same treatment in their personal lives. Emulating the law of grace attracted many unbelievers to Christ because this was an unpopular and baffling response to the trials and buffets of this world. Grace set the believer apart from the common, unbelieving crowd and caused many to wonder the reasons behind such a response. Luke 6:35 details, "But love ye your enemies, and do good, and lend, hoping for nothing again; and your reward shall be great, and ye shall be the children of the Highest: for he is kind unto the unthankful and to the evil." Christ demonstrated a higher standard that was unnatural yet beguiling to a world so ravaged by selfishness and hatred. He willingly loved and taught the people He knew would betray and later crucify Him. Judas Iscariot followed Jesus for His three years of ministry and stood under the grace and love of Christ, yet he still betrayed the Lord for money. The Lord did not expect accolades from those He loved, and His love was unwavering despite the ungrateful hearts of the public. John 1:17 finishes, "For the law was given by Moses, but grace and truth came by Jesus Christ." The Lord Jesus Christ offered so much more than the law ever could and taught an unforgiving and bitter world about a forgiveness and mercy known only through God.

The manner of Jesus' teaching and interactions challenged the world to take heed and consider His unexpected truths and actions, while inspiring many to follow Him. Society and traditions had strained the relationship between God and man to a point where God was portrayed as inaccessible and aloof to the average person; yet the God of the universe drew people to His side and showed an affection, concern, and acceptance that could not be found anywhere else. His authority, love, and godliness inspired His followers to emulate His behavior in their dealings with a lost and dying world in need of redemption.

# CHAPTER III

MADE MORE COMPELLING by His manner, Christ's message intrigued the crowds; the Lord's words did not merely concentrate on the worldly dictates of this life but pointed all who listened to the life beyond this earth. John Sewall notes how Christ's focus did not rest on the temporal evils of His day:

> As if to show the world some external symbol of these inner transformations, Jesus applies his power here and there to some of the ravages of sin. Miracles of mercy radiate from his divine person. He heals the sick. He restores sight to the blind. He gives speech to the dumb, soundness to the cripple, the vigor of health to the palsied. He casts out demons. He calls the dead from the stillness of the tomb. Everywhere his ministry is one of physical restoration as well as of spiritual teaching. Everywhere he shows that he aims not only at the root of sin in the soul, but at the poisonous fruitage of it in the life. The forces of his kingdom, beginning with the

spiritual, would reach out into the physical and secular, would pervade and sweeten every province of life, and would repair the damages that come from sin. The miracles of healing were samples of the complete effect which Christianity would have when in full operation among men. Set up the kingdom, and in time it would carry all other good with it. Seek ye first his kingdom and his righteousness, and all these things shall be added unto you.[28]

Christ did not concentrate on the earthly injustices of the world because that was not His purpose in coming; instead, He directed His audience to the One who could free them from spiritual bondage and lead them to a life of spiritual purpose and prosperity. John 10:10 reveals, "The thief cometh not, but for to steal, and to kill, and to destroy: I am come that they might have life, and that they might have it more abundantly." The message of Christ dynamically convicted the hearts of His audience as He illuminated the life that was prepared to come hereafter. The Lord revealed His identity to the Jews while simultaneously calling them to repentance. Matthew 9:13 reveals, "But go ye and learn what that meaneth, I will have mercy, and not sacrifice: for I am not come to call the righteous, but sinners to repentance." The message of the Lord Jesus Christ disclosed the plan of salvation that had been prepared since the beginning of the world. To ensure the understanding of His audience, Christ explained heavenly principles through earthly relations.

First, earthly interactions were used to communicate the deeper meanings of Christ's teachings to His enraptured audience. John 3:12 queries, "If I have told you earthly things, and ye believe not, how shall ye believe, if I tell you of heavenly things?" In His discourse with Nicodemus, Christ compared the spiritual rebirth to the physical birth required by every person. The Lord used Nicodemus's understanding of physical beginnings to point him to the truths of a spiritual renewing. Dr. Willmington furthers this idea when he declares the need of healing for Nicodemus and all who have been "bitten by sin."[29] Just as Moses was required to raise the brass serpent in the wilderness for the healing of all those who had been bitten by the fiery serpents, so every person must regard the cross and its representation of salvation. Nicodemus understood the implications of this passage; and through this simple comparison, the Lord was able to lead Nicodemus's thinking to his own need for salvation and a spiritual change in his life.

Christ was efficient in His use of temporal considerations to direct His audience's attention to the spiritual message He desired to impart. Luke 12:24 encourages, "Consider the ravens: for they neither sow nor reap; which neither have storehouse nor barn; and God feedeth them: how much more are ye better than the fowls?" The dealings of animals reminded all who listened about the provision of God for His creation. Christ desired for others to ponder the care and plan that the Father extended to the well-being of His children. Luke 12:27 contemplates, "Consider the lilies how they grow: they toil not, they spin not; and yet I say unto you, that Solomon in all his glory was not arrayed like one of these." Christ continued His discourse with the comparison of the lilies clothed in all their beauty to the great riches that Solomon had once boasted of, and yet that powerful king had nothing as valuable as the natural splendor provided to these delicate plants. Matthew Henry notes that Christ's comparison encouraged His disciples to free themselves of the cares and fears that would distract them from the joy and powers offered by a relationship with Christ.[30] The Lord was unwilling for His followers to remove their focus from His great plan for them because they were worried about the trials of this world.

Christ first likened God to an earthly father who sought to provide for the needs of his children. Luke 11:13 reminds, "If ye then, being evil, know how to give good gifts unto your children: how much more shall your heavenly Father give the Holy Spirit to them that ask him?" Comparing the love and provision of an earthly father illuminated the even greater support of a heavenly Father who would always know what was best for His children. Christ encouraged and challenged His audience regarding their relationship with God, and His message equated these earthly principles to the spiritual relationship of man with God that was often misunderstood. Matthew 5:45 exhorts, "That ye may be the children of your Father which is in heaven: for he maketh his sun to rise on the evil and on the good, and sendeth rain on the just and on the unjust." Just as a father rewarded the obedience of his children and punished their disobedience, God the Father behaved in the same manner with His spiritual children. Hebrews 12:7 relays, "If ye endure chastening, God dealeth with you as with sons; for what son is he whom the father chasteneth not?" Jesus presented God the Father differently to demonstrate the necessity of a personal relationship with Him. The disciples and followers of Christ were astounded by these teachings because God had never been posed in such a loving and approachable manner. Matthew 5:48 prompts, "Be ye therefore perfect, even as your Father which is in heaven is perfect." The people were still reminded that their relationship with the Lord had to stem from a change in heart because they could not expect the mercy of God without genuine repentance and modeling after Christ. Heavenly purposes were also revealed through the customary proceedings of the Jewish community.

Christ's discussion and understanding of Jewish customs helped the listeners to better comprehend heavenly principles. Throughout His ministry, the Lord Jesus Christ expertly related newly revealed concepts through His comprehension of the Jews' daily proceedings. Matthew 9:15 reminds, "And Jesus said unto them, Can the children of the bridechamber mourn, as long as the bridegroom is with them? but the days will come, when the bridegroom shall be taken from them, and then shall they fast." The disciples of John and some of the religious leaders questioned the prudence of Christ and His disciples feasting with the publicans and ungodly members of society. Christ's response caused both parties to acknowledge His authority and introduction of unknown principles. Louis A. Barbieri, Jr. noted that Christ and His disciples feasted and rejoiced because the Bridegroom was present.[31] Christ equated the custom of the wedding feasts to His earthly presence and later betrayal; just as the wedding party would faithfully seek the bridegroom's return for his bride and subsequently rejoice in his homecoming, likewise, the followers of Christ would revel in His presence and seek diligently for His arrival to earth.

Utilizing other well-known customs, Jesus Christ demonstrated the need for absolute transformation in the lives of His followers. Matthew 9:16–17 expounds, "No man putteth a piece of new cloth unto an old garment, for that which is put in to fill it up taketh from the garment, and the rent is made worse. Neither do men put new wine into old bottles: else the bottles break, and the wine runneth out, and the bottles perish: but they put new wine into new bottles, and both are preserved." To combine new material with old or to fill broken containers with fresh beverages was both ludicrous and wasteful to the audience of Christ. Matthew Henry notes:

> It was not usual to take a piece of rough woolen cloth, which had never been prepared, to join to an old garment, for it would not join well with the soft, old garment, but would tear it further, and the rent would be made worse. Nor would men put new wine into old leathern bottles, which were going to decay, and would be liable to burst from the fermenting of the wine; but putting the new wine into strong, new, skin bottles, both would be preserved.[32]

The law of grace must be manifested in a combined inward and outward change; if not, the transformation in that life will not be complete. Just as new and old material cannot be effectively blended, neither can a new spirit and an old lifestyle be simultaneously present in the life of a believer. Warren Wiersbe records how the gospel could not be contained in the law because combining the law with grace would create confusion.[33] Christ's offer of new life had to take on a fresh form that was freed from the confines of the law. The law had been established to demonstrate the depravity of man and the great spiritual gulf that separated him from a holy and righteous God. Christ's redemption of man provided a way for them to achieve heaven through His righteousness. The message of Christ contradicted the rituals set down by the Jewish elders.

Traditions that were established by the Jewish leaders were refuted and destroyed in Christ's lessons. Even the hardness of the Israelites regarding certain Old Testament laws was exposed and condemned because they deviated from the true plan of the Scriptures. Mark 10:11–12 contests, "And he saith unto them, Whosoever shall put away his wife, and marry another, committeth adultery against her. And if a woman shall put away her husband, and be married to another, she committeth adultery." Jesus upended the marital status quo of that day when He uttered these fateful words; the Jewish culture was so rife with immorality that husbands and wives were divorcing one another and remarrying with no reasons to back such changes. J. Dwight Pentecost notes that "chastity and marriage were the exception while divorce and immorality were the rule."[34] This was spoken about the Roman culture that was quickly seeping into the Jewish traditions and laws.

Religious leaders were divided on the reasons for a lawful divorce, but all approved of this deviation from the true purpose of marriage. Matthew 19:7–8 continues, "They say unto him, Why did Moses then command to give a writing of divorcement, and to put her away? He saith unto them, Moses because of the hardness of your hearts suffered you to put away your wives: but from the beginning it was not so." Before Jesus' time on earth, the Jews had desired to include divorce within the law written by Moses. This was not the will of God but the will of man because their hearts were hardened to the true example of marriage as set in Genesis. Despite the allowance by the law, divorce was a detestable act, and any person who remarried after was seen as defiled. In Jesus' day, the Jewish culture had made divorce into a natural and easy process that had ultimately destroyed the sanctity of the marriage relationship established by God. Marriage was a spiritual representation of God's connection with His children, and to destroy this relationship through divorce ruined such a portrayal. Christ actively retaught the reason for marriage and stressed its sanctity to His audience.

Another tradition that the Jews had distorted was the Sabbath, as well as the amount of work feasible on this day of rest. Matthew 12:1–8 records:

> At that time Jesus went on the sabbath day through the corn; and his disciples were an hungred, and began to pluck the ears of corn, and to eat. But when the Pharisees saw it, they said unto him, Behold, thy disciples do that which is not lawful to do upon the sabbath day. But he said unto them, Have ye not read what David did, when he was an hungred, and they that were with him; how he entered into the house of God, and did eat the shewbread, which was not lawful for him to eat, neither for them which were with him, but only for the priests? Or have ye not

read in the law, how that on the sabbath days the priests in the temple profane the sabbath, and are blameless? But I say unto you, That in this place is one greater than the temple. But if ye had known what this meaneth, I will have mercy, and not sacrifice, ye would not have condemned the guiltless. For the Son of man is Lord even of the sabbath day.

The religious leaders pounced at the opportunity presented when the disciples ate ears of corn while walking on the Sabbath. These self-righteous men gloated when they assumed that they had caught the Lord in a behavior that would destroy Him, yet the Savior had another lesson to teach. The Pharisees had added many things that could not be done during the Sabbath; these additions, in likewise manner, detracted from the significance and purpose of the day. Christ rebuked the leaders for their hypocritical ways while alerting them to the purpose of worshiping God, and ultimately Him, on the Sabbath.

The additions to the Sabbath were not the only sins committed by the Pharisees. Matthew 23:14 expounds, "Woe unto you, scribes and Pharisees, hypocrites! for ye devour widows' houses, and for a pretence make long prayer: therefore ye shall receive the greater damnation." Jesus denounced the traditional actions of the Pharisees because their religion had long ceased coming from their hearts and instead was just moral actions. They used the traditions and customs of the day to cheat others out of their property and made a pretense of piety through their showy praying in crowded streets. Throughout His ministry, the Lord shared His message of repentance and a need for a personal relationship with God; all these teachings compared earthly subjects with the certainties of heavenly rewards.

Second, heavenly purposes through the illumination of earthly values reigned supreme in the topics of Christ's lectures. Matthew 5:12 encourages, "Rejoice, and be exceeding glad: for great is your reward in heaven: for so persecuted they the prophets which were before you." Christ reminded His followers that they had much to anticipate if they obeyed and patterned their lives after Him. Jesus trained His disciples to focus on the prize instead of the trials that they encountered every day. Matthew 6:20 recommends, "But lay up for yourselves treasures in heaven, where neither moth nor rust doth corrupt, and where thieves do not break through nor steal." Teaching His followers to place more value on heavenly treasures rather than on accumulating gold or prestige emphasized the necessity to live a life worthy of the praise of God. John Sewall recalls how Christ emphasized storing eternal gain and relying on God to supply earthly needs.[35] Every person desires to live a life of comfort and ease, but Jesus did not want His followers to fix their attentions and motives on earthly wealth, for all of it is temporal and will be lost. Heavenly rewards withstand time and destruction, for they are eternal and originate from God. Jesus Christ introduced a new aspect of God to the people listening; God had now become attainable and desirous of a relationship with each person.

The fellowship with God was likened to dealings of man on the earth. The fatherly duties of God were not the only representations presented to the people, for each person was once again apprised of His perfect judgment. The followers of God were encouraged to seek the manner of God and replicate His thinking in their lives. Matthew 18:22–35 demonstrates how Christ's followers were to tailor their philosophy after the ways of God:

> Jesus saith unto him, I say not unto thee, Until seven times: but, Until seventy times seven. Therefore is the kingdom of heaven likened unto a certain king, which would take account of his servants. And when he had begun to reckon, one was brought unto him, which owed him ten thousand talents. But forasmuch as he had not to pay, his lord commanded him to be sold, and his wife, and children, and all that he had, and payment to be made. The servant therefore fell down, and worshipped him, saying, Lord, have patience with me, and I will pay thee all. Then the lord of that servant was moved with compassion, and loosed him, and forgave him the debt. But the same servant went out, and found

Chapter III

one of his fellowservants, which owed him an hundred pence: and he laid hands on him, and took him by the throat, saying, Pay me that thou owest. And his fellowservant fell down at his feet, and besought him, saying, Have patience with me, and I will pay thee all. And he would not: but went and cast him into prison, till he should pay the debt. So when his fellowservants saw what was done, they were very sorry, and came and told unto their lord all that was done. Then his lord, after that he had called him, said unto him, O thou wicked servant, I forgave thee all that debt, because thou desiredst me: Shouldest not thou also have had compassion on thy fellowservant, even as I had pity on thee? And his lord was wroth, and delivered him to the tormentors, till he should pay all that was due unto him. So likewise shall my heavenly Father do also unto you, if ye from your hearts forgive not every one his brother their trespasses.

Peter attempted to assuage his lack of forgiveness by asking the Lord how many times he should forgive his brother's faults. Instead of applauding Peter's fortitude, Jesus demonstrated the need for continual forgiveness toward others since the Father forgives all the sins of each person who repents. Just as the servant was punished for not forgiving his fellow man, so each unforgiving individual would be punished for withholding the same reconciliation found in God.

Forgiveness requires a level of compassion and tolerance more readily demonstrated between family members. Sewall notes that Jesus introduced the fatherhood of God as well as the brotherhood of man.[36] All the rules for good behavior and kindness toward fellow men originated with the teachings of the Bible. Philosophers like Confucius took their ideas from scriptural principles as demonstrated in Proverbs 25:21–22: "If thine enemy be hungry, give him bread to eat; and if he be thirsty, give him water to drink: For thou shalt heap coals of fire upon his head, and the Lord shall reward thee." The Golden Rule can be found within the pages of Scripture, and every philosopher that has existed shares a common ancestry steeped in the teachings of God. Christ constantly reiterated Old Testament teachings about loving each other, whether it be enemies or friends, for the simple purpose of demonstrating God's love for one another. Secular philosophers adopted these godly truths and applied them to their own expectations of a civilized world. These precepts were Christ's earthly reminders that His followers might embrace the heavenly purpose of their creator—to redeem mankind.

The redemption of man was introduced and explained in detail throughout the teachings of the Savior. Lester Reddin notes that God's love for the world led Him to give up His Son that all might live through His sacrifice.[37] God the Father willingly provided His Son as a scapegoat for the sins of the world. This act of love was performed because man was in desperate need of substitutionary atonement. Charles Ryrie explains that man's sinful and spiritually helpless state required a sacrificial substitution.[38] Just as the sacrifices in the Old Testament represented the washing away of sins, so Christ came to be that final substitute and redemption. He was not forced to die for the world, but He willingly offered His life so that many could repent and be redeemed. John 14:6 proclaims, "Jesus saith unto him, I am the way, the truth, and the life: no man cometh unto the Father, but by me." The Lord clearly outlined His claim as the Messiah and the redemption price for all men's sins. Every individual who sought salvation had to follow and trust in the sayings of the Master Teacher. Matthew 4:17 extols, "From that time Jesus began to preach, and to say, Repent: for the kingdom of heaven is at hand." Contrition for sin required the individual to sorrow about their wickedness and turn completely away from committing it again. Such a desperate and drastic dedication portrayed the gravity of each sinner's spiritual condition. Mark 1:15 expresses, "And saying, The time is fulfilled, and the kingdom of God is at hand: repent ye, and believe the gospel." The call for repentance loudly rang through the streets and echoed in the alleys of ancient Israel; many heard it, but not all responded to its plea, yet Christ did not allow this placid response of the people to dampen His drive. John 8:24 reminds, "I said therefore unto you, that ye shall die in your sins: for if ye believe not that I am he, ye shall die in your sins." Every person seeking redemption believed that Christ was the One foretold by the prophets of old. As He admonished, anyone who refused to believe His deity would suffer eternal punishment for their unbelief. Without a disgust and reversal of sinful behavior, people could not enter the eternal bliss of heaven. Each redeemed individual believed and accepted the sacrifice that Christ completed on the cross.

    The heart must change for a person to be redeemed from his sin, and his life would demonstrate this turning from evil. Matthew 7:21 reminds, "Not every one that saith unto me, Lord, Lord, shall enter into the kingdom of heaven; but he that doeth the will of my Father which is in heaven." Many of the religious people of Christ's day found false security in their religion, but Christ alerted them to the need for a change of heart instead of remaining true to their religious dogma. Religion would not and never could save a person from eternal punishment; all Old Testament saints had to have a personal relationship with the Lord. Not all Jews were admitted into paradise because not every Hebrew personally sought after the Lord. Despite their earthly heritage, every Israelite was required to believe in the deity of God and His eventual redemption of man. Their outward actions had to flow from an inward decision to follow Jehovah God. Matthew 10:32–33 challenges, "Whosoever therefore shall confess me before men, him will I confess also before my Father which is in heaven. But whosoever shall deny me before men, him will I also deny before my Father which is in heaven." Redemption from sin was an inward commitment that was later realized through an outward change. The followers of Christ were encouraged to demonstrate their spiritual allegiance to God through their physical actions toward others.

The dynamic teaching of Christ revealed the heavenly treasures and purposes of the Father through the skillful comparison with the dealings of earth. Mankind as a whole failed in understanding the intricate and supernatural mission set down by God the Father. Each person was called to a lifetime ministry of service and sacrifice in the name of Christ, for this was but a small matter in comparison to the ultimate price paid by the Lord. His message called sinners to repentance and illuminated the way for each person to receive redemption; His words brought power and change in every believer's life. The age-old redemption of man offered freedom from sin and purpose in life if a person would but ask and receive the gift of salvation offered from the nail-scarred hands of the Savior.

CHAPTER IV

FURTHERMORE, CHRIST'S didactic and applicable method of teaching ensured the comprehension of His spiritual message. Two centuries later, educational experts have applauded the same techniques observed in the teaching ministry of the Lord Jesus Christ. Many hours of research have been completed and consistently have proven the validity of these learning and teaching practices, and every example demonstrated by Christ's ministry has been deemed the best strategy for imparting knowledge. Dr. Howard Hendricks comments that the methods seen in Christ's teachings "infected" the people who thronged His presence.[39] Jesus Christ demonstrated in multitudes of instances that His teaching methods caught the interest of His audience and directed each person to the truths in His message. His teaching style portrayed His knowledge and authority and has withstood the tests of time. Utilizing imagery and teaching from the known to the unknown, Christ directed His audience to the spiritual truths within His lessons.

First, imagery dominated much of Christ's teaching examples and effectively portrayed the truths of the Scriptures. Creating various scenarios and relating these stories to His audience demonstrated the teaching expertise of the Lord. Matthew 7:26 conveys, "And every one that heareth these sayings of mine, and doeth them not, shall be likened unto a foolish man, which built his house upon the sand." This simple analogy cautioned and foreshadowed the destruction of any person who ignored the words of the Master. His audience understood the practicality of building the proper foundation for a house to be strong enough to withstand the storms and erosion of nature; applying this principle of a strong spiritual foundation to each life was made easy because Christ caused His listener to visualize the problem needing to be fixed. Robert Marzano, a leading educator in research-based teaching strategies, asserts that one of the purposes of teaching is to establish mental pictures in the minds of students.[40] Once this is accomplished, scholars will recall the lessons previously taught when faced with similar struggles at later times in life. These mental pictures will effectively remind each person of the correct response for each future situation. Christ ensured that His audience had clear representations of the topics He introduced to them. Matthew 18:23 relates, "Therefore is the kingdom of heaven likened unto a certain king, which would take account of his servants." Once again, the people of Jesus' day would have quickly connected to this simile since it dealt with common factors of their time. They understood that a king required his servants to give an account of all their dealings while he was absent; the servants would receive a blessing or punishment based on their performance while their master was gone. Likewise, the kingdom of heaven required the followers of the Messiah to faithfully serve in His absence while expecting His imminent return from heaven. The audience of Christ effectively listened to His teaching and recorded His principles within their hearts for the time when they believed His words for themselves.

Christ generated these various mental pictures because He recognized that these representations would remain with His audience long after His earthly presence was absent. Robert Marzano also proves that these nonlinguistic representations add another layer of understanding that ensure students can properly relate to the information provided for them.[41] Allowing students to connect to abstract principles ensures successful understanding and application in the learning process. Christ constantly implemented these techniques within His ministry during His pursuit of relaying spiritual truth and healing to a lost and dying world. Matthew 25:1 continues, "Then shall the kingdom of heaven be likened unto ten virgins, which took their lamps, and went forth to meet the bridegroom." Using the comparison of a known tradition regarding the marriage ceremony, Christ impressed upon His audience the need to be ready for the coming of the eternal

King, just as the wedding party was to prepare for the return of the bridegroom. Larry Pettegrew also notes that it was a common custom for the doors of the banquet hall to be locked once the entire bridal party had entered and for those doors to remain locked throughout the ceremony.[42] Christ masterfully compared the coming of the kingdom of God to this special moment in Jewish customs; for when the Lord returns, all believers shall be taken with Him, but those who seem to follow Christ yet are unprepared in their hearts because of their unbelief shall be left behind. The Jews present in His ministry related to this tradition and left with the truths of the coming kingdom hidden within their hearts. Imagery in His teaching was not the only way Christ demonstrated key educational methods, for He also exhibited spiritual truths through His miracles and demonstrations of power.

Miracles showed the deity of Christ to all who could see or hear of His great works. As any great teacher could relate, Christ did not merely rely on His words to show His lessons to His audience; instead, His words were supported by His many miracles. John 12:18 conveys, "For this cause the people also met him, for that they heard that he had done this miracle." The crowds were drawn by the power and wonder presented through the miracles performed by the Lord while on earth. His actions captivated His audience while also teaching valuable truths about Himself and salvation as they watched in astonishment. Braley and his associates comment that interactive learning requires internal and external stimulations to provide the desired results in education.[43] Christ utilized this type of learning within His own lessons because His words worked on the inner understanding while His mighty deeds demonstrated the truth of His remarks. The audience of Christ received a fully intrinsic and extrinsic education; and as a result, many believed in the deity of their Teacher. Mark 2:5–12 records one of the greatest miracles Christ performed during His earthly ministry:

> When Jesus saw their faith, he said unto the sick of the palsy, Son, thy sins be forgiven thee. But there were certain of the scribes sitting there, and reasoning in their hearts, Why doth this man thus speak blasphemies? who can forgive sins but God only? And immediately when Jesus perceived in his spirit that they so reasoned within themselves, he said unto them, Why reason ye these things in your hearts? Whether is it easier to say to the sick of the palsy, Thy sins be forgiven thee; or to say, Arise, and take up thy bed, and walk? But that ye may know that the Son of man hath power on earth to forgive sins, (he saith to the sick of the palsy,) I say unto thee, Arise, and take up thy bed, and go thy way into thine house. And immediately he arose, took up the bed, and went forth before them all; insomuch that they were all amazed,

and glorified God, saying, We never saw it on this fashion.

Many instances throughout Scripture, the learned priests and religious leaders marveled at the power demonstrated by Jesus through His healing power. Though they should have immediately recognized that His supremacy was granted by God, they scoffed and even accused the Lord of being a worker of the devil. Yet Christ's actions caused many to believe and accept His gift of salvation, for His miracles portrayed the greatness of their God and revealed that the Messiah had arrived. Christ performed many miracles for the crowds to witness and share far and wide, yet the Scriptures record several instances where the Lord privately demonstrated His power to His disciples in a personal rebuttal of the accusations from His enemies.

Demonstrations of His power refuted the false claims of His accusers who would have put Him to death if they had the authority to kill the Son of God. Matthew 14:25–33 records a powerful demonstration of Christ's sovereignty:

> And in the fourth watch of the night Jesus went unto them, walking on the sea. And when the disciples saw him walking on the sea, they were troubled, saying, It is a spirit; and they cried out for fear. But straightway Jesus spake unto them, saying, Be of good cheer; it is I; be not afraid. And Peter answered

him and said, Lord, if it be thou, bid me come unto thee on the water. And he said, Come. And when Peter was come down out of the ship, he walked on the water, to go to Jesus. But when he saw the wind boisterous, he was afraid; and beginning to sink, he cried, saying, Lord, save me. And immediately Jesus stretched forth his hand, and caught him, and said unto him, O thou of little faith, wherefore didst thou doubt? And when they were come into the ship, the wind ceased. Then they that were in the ship came and worshipped him, saying, Of a truth thou art the Son of God.

Modern educators have continually stressed the importance of demonstrating knowledge instead of simply verbalizing information; these principles can be observed in the many interactions of Christ with the people of His day. John Milton Gregory once expounded upon this idea: "Knowledge cannot be passed like a material substance from one mind to another, for thoughts are not objects which may be held and handled…. Ideas must be rethought, experience must be re-experienced."[44] True learning is accomplished through mentally and physically examining the truths presented; scholars will finally have explored the laws provided and demonstrated their validity through investigation. Marzano points out that testing theories heightens the learning experience because students can observe previously taught principles in a practical application.[45]

Education should not merely be composed of verbal conveyance; but to be successful in imparting knowledge, teaching must also include moments of personal investigation.

The disciples were introduced to the deity of Christ on several different occasions; and as a result, their faith was heightened as they slowly understood the identity of the Lord. The Savior repetitively showed His true self to His followers because He knew that once was not enough for His disciples to realize whom they were observing. Mark 4:39 records, "And he arose, and rebuked the wind, and said unto the sea, Peace, be still. And the wind ceased, and there was a great calm." Astonished reactions were prevalent among the disciples, but Christ persevered in His demonstrations of His authority because He understood that His followers needed to know exactly whom they were believing. Matthew 17:1–5 records the moment of transfiguration and God the Father's claim of His Son:

> And after six days Jesus taketh Peter, James, and John his brother, and bringeth them up into an high mountain apart, and was transfigured before them: and his face did shine as the sun, and his raiment was white as the light. And, behold, there appeared unto them Moses and Elias talking with him. Then answered Peter, and said unto Jesus, Lord, it is good for us to be here: if thou wilt, let us make here three tabernacles; one for

thee, and one for Moses, and one for Elias. While he yet spake, behold, a bright cloud overshadowed them: and behold a voice out of the cloud, which said, This is my beloved Son, in whom I am well pleased; hear ye him.

Moments like the transfiguration and resurrection solidified the deity of Christ and imparted a certainty of His identity to His disciples. Both instances were quite private moments between the Lord and His closest followers, yet each of these times demonstrated the unquestionable truth of Christ's sovereignty and was shared with every person who would listen. The Lord understood that His disciples sometimes needed to see with their human eyes as well as to comprehend in their hearts the absolute undeniability of His messages. Modern teachers have applied this same concept to their educational strategies because all students must be able to see as much as they can to fully understand the various principles taught in school. The demonstrations and miracles of the Lord Jesus Christ were implemented throughout His teachings for the sole purpose of comparing previously known material with new concepts presented within His ministry.

Second, He masterfully taught from the known lessons of the law to the unknown concepts of grace and redemption. Modern educational experts have agreed that teaching unfamiliar concepts through identifying similarities and differences is a crucial part of excellent teaching. Larry Pettegrew furthers this perception when he comments that the best learning comes from comparing new material with previous experiences and applying that knowledge to the present.[46] Christ accomplished this teaching method throughout His ministry, and His lessons still reach the lives of people existing centuries after His earthly mission was completed. Marzano attests that through various methods of comparison, teachers can create situations where their students are required to think through problems and find the solutions on their own.[47] Christ expertly demonstrated this specific technique throughout His earthly teaching career. Using various daily activities, Jesus related much of the spiritual realm to the everyday life of His audience; He would then ask leading questions in an endeavor to stimulate the reasoning and understanding of His audience.

Using the day-to-day events of His time, Christ continually challenged His audience in a manner that was relative to their lives. Gary L. Cate notes that in an appealing presentation of the unknown, Christ invited His disciples to "take my yoke upon you, and learn of me."[48] His disciples understood the need for sameness and cooperation for a yoke of oxen to work at maximum capacity, and Christ used this analogy to help His followers further comprehend the necessity to share the same mindset with the Savior they had pledged to follow. The Lord knew that His disciples had to be of one accord with Him and with their spiritual brethren; therefore, Jesus pressed this importance upon His followers because

Chapter IV

He knew that His time on earth was quickly dissipating and that His comrades needed to be prepared for that day when He would return to heaven. Therefore, He taught with parables and leading questions that presented His message in an understandable and memorable manner.

One way in which Christ taught the unknown was found through parables that quickly related heavenly principles to His audience. Parables are still employed in modern society because they are such an intriguing and effective method of imparting knowledge. Matthew 13:10–13 discloses the reasons behind why Christ used parables within His teaching style:

> And the disciples came, and said unto him, Why speakest thou unto them in parables? He answered and said unto them, Because it is given unto you to know the mysteries of the kingdom of heaven, but to them it is not given. For whosoever hath, to him shall be given, and he shall have more abundance: but whosoever hath not, from him shall be taken away even that he hath. Therefore speak I to them in parables: because they seeing see not; and hearing they hear not, neither do they understand.

Parables revealed hard spiritual truths in an often fun yet unforgettable manner that ensured the understanding from the various backgrounds represented within the multitude. While at the time many of His audience did not understand everything He communicated to them, the parables and their timeless truths remained with those that listened and were manifested at opportune moments within each heart. Matthew 13:24 continues, "Another parable put he forth unto them, saying, The kingdom of heaven is likened unto a man which sowed good seed in his field." Through parables, Christ explained heavenly truths regarding salvation and godly living while also giving His audience a chance to apply these principles to their lives. Each parable was relevant to present living as well as influential in training spiritual thinkers and people who could discern the Scriptures. Simon J. Kistemaker illuminates that the open-ended parables of the Lord required His audience to decide their own ending for each problem presented within these literary masterpieces.[49] Most parables ended with a question or in ambiguity so each person could employ the relevant information to their unique circumstances and experiences. This methodology encouraged His audience to ponder on the problems presented and determine what would be the correct response.

Modern educators are encouraged to employ this same principle to their teaching for the stimulation of independent thought and future application by their students. Teaching should include much more than rote memorization and regurgitation of facts and should instead reach the heart of each student as they seek to apply its wisdom. Michael

J. Anthony corroborates this idea when he states that Jesus' teaching stimulated serious meditation and reflection from His audience.[50] Christ understood that true learning is based on comprehension and application of the principles taught. Merely reciting required facts and answers fails to demonstrate true understanding and deceives untrained individuals in believing that their students have really learned the material. Pettegrew details how Christ used "problems" to teach His disciples and audience about spiritual truths.[51] The dilemmas of the world enabled the Lord to illuminate His solution and liberation from the effects of sin because the desperate cry of the multitude led many to seek the One who could defeat their greatest fears and teach them of novel and redeeming spiritual truths. Parables provided the perfect gateway to later questioning and discussion regarding the ideas Christ presented in His lessons.

Christ posed a myriad of questions that caused His followers to eventually discover the truth for themselves. The Lord is often recorded within the Scriptures holding sessions where He answered and asked questions with His audience and disciples. Questions were used to determine the level of comprehension represented within His audience. Matthew 16:13–15 attests, "When Jesus came into the coasts of Caesarea Philippi, he asked his disciples, saying, Whom do men say that I the Son of man am? And they said, Some say that thou art John the Baptist: some, Elias; and others, Jeremias, or one of the prophets. He saith unto them, But whom say ye that I am?" Every succession of questions had a distinct purpose of generating individual thought and consideration of the lessons presented daily. The Lord encouraged inquiries and independent research among the crowd that gathered at His feet because Christ knew each person had to make a conscious choice to believe and apply His truths regarding salvation, sin, and a relationship with God the Father. J. Paul Martin observes that "critical thinking requires understanding and action, not just following the rules."[52] Modern educators realize this and strongly advocate for students to be taught in a manner that drives students to discover the truth for themselves and prove this understanding through various projects and assignments. Applying the content of His lessons allowed the students of Christ to see the truth behind His words within their own lives.

The Master Teacher desired for His followers to listen to the teachings He presented, but He also required personal application of learned material. His questions were always necessary and had a definite purpose that would later draw out the comprehension stored in the hearts of His believers. Matthew 16:16 concludes, "And Simon Peter answered and said, Thou art the Christ, the Son of the living God." Peter demonstrated his understanding and application through his answer to the questions put forth by the Lord. The disciples were required to acknowledge their fervency and emulate their lives after Jesus Christ. James Braley and his associates note that teachers need "to guide the student in the process of making sense out of the new knowledge or skills; to use it; to fit it in; to store it."[53] The Master Teacher led His audience to the root of the problem and expertly guided them to discovering the truth on their own; by doing this, Christ ensured that His followers truly understood the lessons He wanted to impart to them. The Master could definitively defend His teaching style through the proof that His objectives were being met by the understanding demonstrated in His students' lives.

The teachings of Christ developed the spiritual learning and independence required for His disciples' future ministries. John Milton Gregory notes, "The true function of the teacher is to create the most favorable conditions for self-learning.... True teaching is not that which gives knowledge, but that which stimulates pupils to gain it. One might say that he teaches best who teaches least."[54] The Lord embraced this principle as He instigated the continual training of His disciples and the early church members. Throughout His ministry, Christ reiterated much of the Old Testament and answered questions regarding the laws established in the days of Moses; very few times did Jesus teach something utterly unrelated to already established truths. He illuminated passages that had grown neglected through the centuries, but His methods required His audience to apply the content of His message within their own lives. To this day, Christ encourages

His believers to seek the Word of God and faithfully live according to its commandments. The Scriptures constantly attest to this requirement of teaching, and the Lord masterfully incorporated this technique throughout the various stages of His ministry.

Teaching methodology has affected the success of imparting knowledge since the beginning of time, and educators have spent countless hours and resources endeavoring to discover the best techniques required to divulge permanent understanding. The lessons, mannerisms, and interactions of the Lord Jesus Christ's earthly ministry demonstrated a masterful application of the best practices for effectively transferring knowledge. John Milton Gregory once observed, "It is the teacher's mission... by sympathy, by example, and by every means of influence—by objects for the senses, by facts for the intelligence—to excite the mind of the pupils, to stimulate their thoughts.... The greatest of teachers said: 'The seed is the word.' The true teacher stirs the ground and sows the seed."[55] Much can be gleaned from the ministry of the Lord and integrated in the teaching careers of secular and Christian educators; students must be encouraged to seek the truth through the daily practices of educators. Christ's teaching method is still being applied in the classroom and has been proved to be the most beneficial in the permanent retention of knowledge.

Chapter V

PREVIOUS CHAPTERS HAVE discussed how Christ's masterful teaching revealed the effect that His manner, message, and method held over His audience; now these four principles shall be applied to the lives of His modern disciples. The Lord understood His audience and implemented various manners and methods to effectively share His message of salvation with all nations of the earth. Dr. Howard Hendricks once described, "As an effective teacher, you must not only know that which you would teach—that is, your content—but you must also know those whom you wish to teach. You are not interested simply in inculcating principles; you want to infect people. Therefore, the way people learn determines how you teach. This is the Law of Education."[56] Throughout His earthly ministry, Christ exemplified this law of education and instructed His followers to teach and spread the gospel to the whole world.

The evangelization of the church age prevailed through the known world and "infected" all who believed its biblical truths. Soon the whole known world had heard of the Messiah and His saving power; this news is still shared across the world to lands and people who have not yet been affected by its healing might. Matthew 9:35 relays, "And Jesus went about all the cities and villages, teaching in their synagogues, and preaching the gospel of the kingdom, and healing every sickness and every disease among the people." Even in His lifetime, the Lord demonstrated the need and effectiveness of salvation; His disciples learned how to spread the gospel through the example of Jesus. Homer Kent, Jr. comments that Christ trained His disciples to teach and share the gospel with the world.[57] Likewise, His disciples demonstrated these truths with other believers and stressed the gravity of educating the world about the Savior. To this day, Christians are expected to share the gospel through their personal lives and public ministries.

First, the principles found in the earthly ministry of Christ should be demonstrated through the private lives of believers. Christians have often forgotten that their lives exist for the sole purpose of bringing glory to God; instead, many American believers, especially, have relaxed into the comfortable lives afforded to them through the freedom of this modern age. The desperate struggle between eternal life and eternal damnation has been subdued by the roaring cry of materialism. Dr. Hendricks recalls a conversation he once had with a man declaring to be a Christian:

A man tells me he's a Christian businessman, and he cheats. I ask him how he accounts for that in terms of Christian principles. "Hendricks," he says, "you don't understand. We are in Rome! And the verse says, 'When in Rome, do as the Romans do.'" "Say, I've got another verse for you," I tell him. "When in Rome as a Christian, don't do as the Romans do."[58]

Materialism and its ilk are often treated as recent calamities of the modern age; yet this same dilemma prevailed in the time of Christ. Christians and nonbelievers struggled with a desire for gain and prosperity; hence, Paul instructed new believers to remove themselves from their old lifestyles, for they had been transformed into new creatures through Christ. The inward actions of a believer must be demonstrated through the drastic changes in the outward behavior of a man who has been newly introduced to the healing power of Christ. II Corinthians 5:17 expounds, "Therefore if any man be in Christ, he is a new creature: old things are passed away; behold, all things are become new." Christians must have a personal life that exudes the influence of the Lord and adheres to His teachings. The old ways of the flesh ought not to dominate the thoughts and actions of the believer who has been gloriously rescued from the clutches of sin. Matthew Henry notes that the saved individual is given a new heart upon salvation.[59] This new nature compels the believer to follow the Lord and apply His principles in every area of life. Matthew 4:23 discloses, "And Jesus went about all Galilee, teaching in their synagogues, and preaching the gospel of the kingdom, and healing all manner of sickness and all manner of disease among the people." Just as the Savior healed the bodily sick and changed their physical lives, saved individuals should live differently from the throngs of unredeemed people who surround them every day. John Louis A. Barbieri, Jr. notes that this passage reveals the identity and purpose of the Lord Jesus Christ.[60] Christians should follow His example, as they have an important identity and purpose as laid out by the Father. The private actions and thoughts of a believer will be manifested through the outward activities that can be observed by the world.

The personal walk of a Christian should be permeated with the godliness and love of Christ. Believers should interact in a manner that clearly directs the attention of the world to the Savior who made eternal life possible; thus, every Christian must emulate the Lord in their private behavior. Dr. Hendricks notes that "what you are is far more important than what you say or do."[61] The internal motives of each person far outweigh the outward perception of an individual since these attributes lend authenticity to everything done in the presence of others. Christ drew the crowds to His side because He offered a sincerity and truth that the world needed and sorely lacked. Matthew 4:25

describes, "And there followed him great multitudes of people from Galilee, and from Decapolis, and from Jerusalem, and from Judaea, and from beyond Jordan." People from many walks of life sought Christ because He differed greatly from the pompous religious leaders of the day. Louis Barbieri, Jr. also comments that the ministry of the Lord and His followers was dramatic for the crowds that thronged their presence.[62] Every Christian should search his own life to determine whether his life reflects the same magnitude as their Savior and His first disciples. The personal life of Christ was characterized by His constant devotion to the heavenly Father through prayer and His unwavering concern and care for the souls lost in the darkness.

Prayer strengthened the Lord throughout His ministry and set a precedent for all believers to follow. Matthew 14:23 notes, "And when he had sent the multitudes away, he went up into a mountain apart to pray: and when the evening was come, he was there alone." Throughout Scripture, the Lord is recorded to seek His Father in prayer and to accomplish this on His own. Prayer demonstrates a personal relationship between a believer and his Lord and can only be accomplished on a personal level. Each believer must pray for himself to receive the blessings provided through this special communication; no one can expect the prayers of others to strengthen their own relationship with the Savior. Prayer was crucial to the life and ministry of the Lord, and He shared this vital relationship with His disciples when He taught them how to address their heavenly Father. Luke 11:1 reveals, "And it came to pass, that, as he was praying in a certain place, when he ceased, one of his disciples said unto him, Lord, teach us to pray, as John also taught his disciples." The prayer of righteous people is treasured by the Lord, and He will answer their plea. Matthew 26:36 records, "Then cometh Jesus with them unto a place called Gethsemane, and saith unto the disciples, Sit ye here, while I go and pray yonder." The Lord taught His disciples how to pray through His own example of prayer, but He would not force them to pray with Him even when He called on His Father before His death. While the Lord prayed, the disciples slept, thus demonstrating that prayer is a personal decision and cannot be forced on any individual. The closer the Lord drew to His Father, the more in tune He was to the plans and wishes of God the Father. Matthew 26:39 entreats, "And he went a little further, and fell on his face, and prayed, saying, O my Father, if it be possible, let this cup pass from me: nevertheless not as I will, but as thou wilt." Even in the greatest distress of His earthly ministry, Christ willingly chose to adhere to the death of the cross though His soul was anguished and His body suffered the consequences. Louis Barbieri, Jr. observes that the agony the Lord suffered during this prayer was most likely caused by His imminent separation from the Father and contact with sin.[63] Each Christian should examine their life and determine whether their soul shrivels when they are absent from the Father and surrounded by sin; for until this sentiment is felt, the believer will not experience true fellowship with their heavenly Father. Godliness must permeate the inner workings of a Christian for their outward actions to reflect the power and love of Christ.

The devotion of Christ was exemplified by the pure and unwavering care that the Lord demonstrated to the world when He sacrificed Himself on the cross. John 3:16 details, "For God so loved the world, that he gave his only begotten Son, that whosoever believeth in him should not perish, but have everlasting life." The sacrificial love of the God of creation must be demonstrated in the personal walk of every Christian. The believers of Christ have remained on the earth for the principal purpose of spreading the salvation truths found in the Word of God. Just as Christ spent His earthly ministry in the pursuit of bringing lost souls into the fold of God, so the life of every Christian should be aimed toward this same goal. Luke 7:13 notes, "And when the Lord saw her, he had compassion on her, and said unto her, Weep not." Christ's ministry was not characterized by just physical healing, but every action He took illuminated the need for a spiritual awakening in the life of every person with whom He came into contact. Warren Wiersbe notes that Christ raised Lazarus from the dead because He loved him, and it brought glory to God the Father.[64] Every action of the Lord glorified the Father and revealed the identity of the Son to the world; Christ desired to divulge the love of the Father to the world and lead the lost of Israel to the Good Shepherd. John 15:9 reminds, "As the Father hath loved me, so have I loved you: continue ye in my love." The disciples were exhorted to follow the example of their Lord and demonstrate His eternal care to the lost souls of the world. Even today, Christians must pattern their lives after the Master Teacher and illuminate the darkness through their personal relationship with Him.

The way Christians converse with others should be so distinctive and alluring that the world will be drawn to the Savior. Jesus Christ spoke in a manner that astonished and intrigued the people of His day. Matthew 7:28 details, "And it came to pass, when Jesus had ended these sayings, the people were astonished at his doctrine." His speech differed greatly from the average person because His topic was not of this world; even the religious leaders of His day did not converse the way He did because only His words held life. Many religious organizations have claimed to follow Christ, yet they have muddied the spiritual waters with their traditions and counterfeit measures. Sadly, many people have been harmed and scarred by these false religions claiming Christ as their master. The truth should be obvious because of its stark contrast to the lies, and every Christian's speech should drastically differ from the common and vulgar language of this world and its counterfeits. Mark 10:24 expounds, "And the disciples were astonished at his words. But Jesus answereth again, and saith unto them, Children, how hard is it for them that trust in riches to enter into the kingdom of God." Even the believers of His day were shocked by the difference of Christ's doctrine and speech; this was precisely the manner in which unsaved counterparts should react to the believers' adherence to the example of the Lord Jesus Christ. Luke 2:47 emphasizes, "And all that heard him were astonished at his understanding and answers." The Lord had a great knowledge of the Scriptures, and every believer should also demonstrate this same level of knowledge regarding the principles of the Bible. Luke 4:32 notes, "And they were astonished at his doctrine: for his word was with power." Every Christian should teach with confidence because the words of the Bible exude a power and authority that no earthly or spiritual influence can rival. Philippians 2:10 asserts, "That at the name of Jesus every knee should bow, of things in heaven, and things in earth, and things under the earth." People are compelled to submit when the name of Christ is used because His name is far above any name ever created. Matthew Henry comments, "At the name of Jesus, not the mere sound of the word, but the authority of Jesus, all should pay solemn homage. It is to the glory of God the Father, to confess that Jesus Christ is Lord; for it is his will, that all men should honour the Son as they honour the Father, John v. 23."[65] The personal life of every Christian ought to draw each sinner to the foot of the cross and ultimately into the arms of his Savior.

Second, the professional lives of Christians should portray the truths in Christ's earthly teachings. Each Christian has a personal duty to align their life with the Savior because they have a public ministry with each person they meet. Charles Ryrie notes that the responsibility of the church is to teach both their congregation and the surrounding community.[66] Teaching is a gift from God, but it is also a learned ability that can and should be present in the ministry of every believer. This responsibility has also been mirrored within the Great Commission and clearly was established that all the world would be changed by the gospel. Matthew 28:19 commands, "Go ye therefore, and teach all nations, baptizing them in the name of the Father, and of the Son, and of the Holy Ghost." The Lord desired each of His followers to demonstrate this character trait within their public ministries for the intent purpose of directing others to salvation. The Lord certainly had not required something of His disciples that was not also a constant within His own ministry. Homer A. Kent, Jr. observes, "Whether on a mountainside, or sitting in a boat, or lecturing in a synagogue, or merely walking along the road, teaching was the outstanding characteristic of Jesus during the days of his ministry."[67] No matter the location, Jesus Christ taught the people surrounding Him; He was never shy or hesitant about introducing every person to His Father. The

Chapter V

church was established upon the precept that the entire world was to be reached by the gospel regardless of nationality or earthly ties. Mark 13:10 states, "And the gospel must first be published among all nations." Christians were instructed to share the salvation message throughout the world by teaching and preaching. Acts 2:42 relays, "And they continued stedfastly in the apostles' doctrine and fellowship, and in breaking of bread, and in prayers." The apostles followed the directives laid down by the Lord through teaching these same truths to the Christians and churches established throughout the known world. This was accomplished by every believer teaching their lost community while performing their daily tasks.

Christians should treat those at their workplaces with the love and concern that Christ demonstrated for all the people that He encountered. Matthew 20:34 describes, "So Jesus had compassion on them, and touched their eyes: and immediately their eyes received sight, and they followed him." Regardless of the identity of each person, Christ demonstrated His love for them as He healed their bodies and changed their lives. Christ did not stand in judgment for the sins ever present in the hearts of His audience, and He was not afraid to touch them and alter their spiritual condition. Mark 1:41 records, "And Jesus, moved with compassion, put forth his hand, and touched him, and saith unto him, I will; be thou clean." No matter how filthy their situation was, the Lord loved and saved and taught each person as if they were the only one to live on this earth.

Jesus continued His ministry through His encouragement and lessons concerning the good deeds wrought in each life. Mark 5:19 details, "Howbeit Jesus suffered him not, but saith unto him, Go home to thy friends, and tell them how great things the Lord hath done for thee, and hath had compassion on thee." The individuals who changed the most had the greatest influence on the lives of their friends and families because they demonstrated the power of Christ. Mark 6:34 continues, "And Jesus, when he came out, saw much people, and was moved with compassion toward them, because they were as sheep not having a shepherd: and he began to teach them many things." Jesus Christ's ministry demonstrated how He taught all those willing to listen to His instruction and who desired a personal change. Many Christians have stated that people no longer wish to hear the salvation message, and many individuals have responded viciously to the attempts of Christians in teaching the gospel to them. Dr. Hendricks once recounted a conversation he had: "When I first moved to Texas many years ago, I once quoted the saying, 'You can lead a horse to water, but you can't make him drink.' A tall West Texan answered back, 'Son, you're wrong. You can feed him salt.'"[68] What a wonderful reminder to every soul-winner who has been wearied by the continual refusal of the lost; the life of a believer witnesses far better than any words of any language. Matthew 5:13 exhorts, "Ye are the salt of the earth: but if the salt have lost his savour, wherewith shall it be salted? it is thenceforth good for nothing, but to be cast out, and to be trodden under foot of men." The gospel is sometimes hindered by the unsavory life of the Christian, and many unbelievers have refused salvation for this very reason. Matthew Henry details the utter need for Christians to have their lives patterned after the ministry of the Master Teacher:

> The example of our Lord Jesus Christ is set before us. We must resemble him in his life, if we would have the benefit of his death.—Notice the two natures of Christ; his Divine nature, and human nature. Who being in the form of God, partaking in the Divine nature, as the eternal and only-begotten Son of God had not thought it a robbery to be equal with God, and to receive Divine worship from men. His human nature; herein he became like us in all things except sin. Thus low, of his own will, he stooped from the glory he had with the Father before the world was.—Christ's two states, of humiliation and exaltation, are noticed. Christ not only took upon him the likeness and fashion, or form of a man, but of one in poverty and suffering. But the lowest step was his dying the death of the cross, the death of a malefactor and a slave; exposed to public hatred and scorn.—The exaltation was

of Christ's human nature, in union with the Divine.... How we see such motives to self-denying love as nothing else can supply. Do we thus love and obey the Son of God?[69]

Every follower must emulate their life after the Savior and interact with their fellow man just as He did; this is the only way for the world to be saved from the depravity that has ensnared it. The way a Christian communicates will determine whether the lost will listen to or ignore the salvation message.

Christians should communicate in a way that convicts and encourages those that they work with to listen to the truth of the Scriptures. Dr. Harold Willmington notes that God gives each Christian special abilities that they can later use when witnessing to the unsaved.[70] Jesus promised to send a helper to His disciples as He was preparing them for His death and imminent return to glory. The Holy Spirit was that comforter and has enabled every Christian to complete the task set down by the Father. Dr. Howard Hendricks extols each believer to live a life of joy and to demonstrate this excitement through their conversation.[71] Each Christian should feel the message that they are presenting to the world, yet many times the believer can be so discouraged that it is impossible for them to share any joy or comfort with the lost around them. At times, this difference will cause the world to reject Christians, but no one can accurately deny the truths found within the Scriptures. John 15:18 describes, "If the world hate you, ye know that it hated me before it hated you." Even though the Lord was despised by His enemies, Jesus did not waver in His earthly purpose and continually sought the world's redemption, regardless that it culminated in His death. If the Lord could live in such a manner when He knew of His earthly end, no disciple of Christ can honestly complain about the treatment given to them by the world. John 8:38 explains, "I speak that which I have seen with my Father: and ye do that which ye have seen with your father." Christians have a spiritual heritage with the Father and should be sharing the truths of their spiritual parentage with the lost world. The heavenly Father has desired for every soul to repent and return into the perfect relationship once known by man in the beginning. Matthew Henry observes that the testimony of the Christian is strengthened when following the Word of God becomes a natural occurrence instead of a duty to be performed.[72] The inward thoughts of a man will determine his speech and manner of living; a pure testimony will only result from a godly lifestyle and heart. The speech of believers must demonstrate a drastic difference between the world and the Father who seeks reconciliation with His creation.

Christians, regardless of occupation or talent, have much to apply from the ministry of the Master Teacher regarding His audience, manner, method, and message. The Lord faithfully demonstrated the need for teaching others about salvation and a fulfilling life of service while on this earth. Many

Christians can be hesitant at accomplishing this great mission, whether it be because of uncertainty or fear of the unknown. Continually, the Scriptures urge the believers of Christ to train more servants and teach them and the world about the life God has always intended for His creation. Once every Christian has embraced this crucial purpose, the world can be changed and introduced to the Savior who sacrificed all in the pursuit of men's souls. Matthew 25:23 exhorts, "His lord said unto him, Well done, good and faithful servant; thou hast been faithful over a few things, I will make thee ruler over many things: enter thou into the joy of thy lord." May every believer strive to hear those words when each man stands before the throne of God and receives the judgment for his earthly dealings. Emulating the principles demonstrated in the earthly teaching ministry of the Master Teacher should be the goal of every Christian while on this earth.

Bibliography

Anthony, Michael J. 2001. *Christian Education: Foundations for the Twenty-first Century.* Grand Rapids, Michigan: Baker Academic.

Braley, James, Jack Layman, and Ray White, eds. 2003. *Foundations of Christian School Education.* Colorado Springs: Purposeful Design Publications.

Cate, Gary L. 1967. "Christ as Teacher." *Central Bible Quarterly* 10: 4. https://www.galaxie.com/article/cenq10-4-04?highlight=Master%20teacher.

Chilton, Bruce. 2015. "The Gospel According to John's Rabbi Jesus." *Bulletin for Biblical Research* 25: 1. https://www.galaxie.com/article/bbr25-1-04?highlight=Master%20teacher.

Hendricks, Dr. Howard. 1987. *Teaching to Change Lives.* New York: Penguin Random House.

Henry, Matthew. 1987. *Matthew Henry's Concise Commentary.* Chicago: Moody Press.

Kent, Jr., Homer A. 1980. "A Time to Teach." *Grace Theological Journal* 01: 1. https://www.galaxie.

com/article/gtj01-1-02?highlight=Master%20teacher.

Kistemaker, Simon J. 2005. "Jesus As Story Teller: Literary Perspectives On The Parables." *Masters Seminary Journal* 16: 1. https://www.galaxie.com/article/tmsj16-1-03?highlight=Master%20teacher.

Martin, J. P. 2007. "Christ in the Classroom." *Commonweal* 134: 7. https://www.proquest.com/magazines/christ-classroom/docview/210404896/se-2?accountid=170150.

Marzano, Robert J., Debra Pickering, and Jane E. Pollock. 2001. *Classroom Instruction that Works*. Virginia: Association for Supervision and Curriculum Development.

Pentecost, J. Dwight. 1981. *The Words and Works of Jesus Christ*. Grand Rapids: Zondervan.

Pettegrew, Larry D. 1972. "Teaching Principles of Christ." *Central Bible Quarterly* 15:1. https://www.galaxie.com/article/cenq15-1-01?highlight=Master%20teacher.

Pettegrew, Larry D. 1972. "Teaching Methods of Christ." *Central Bible Quarterly* 15:2. https://www.galaxie.com/article/cenq15-2-01?highlight=Master%20teacher.

Reddin, Lester. 1912. "Jesus the Rabbi." *Bibliotheca Sacra* 069: 276. https://www.galaxie.com/

article/bsac069-276-08?highlight=Master%20teacher.

Ryrie, Charles C. 1999. *Basic Theology*. California: The Lockman Foundation.

Sewall, John S. 1895. "The Social Ethics of Jesus." *Bibliotheca Sacra* 052: 206. https://www.galaxie.com/article/bsac052-206-04?highlight=Master%20teacher.

Walvoord, John F. and Roy B. Zuck. 1984. *The Bible Knowledge Commentary: New Testament*. Colorado Springs: David Cook Distribution.

Walvoord, John F. and Roy B. Zuck. 1985. *The Bible Knowledge Commentary: Old Testament*. Colorado Springs: David Cook Distribution.

Wiersbe, Warren W. 1992. *Wiersbe's Expository Outlines on the New Testament*. Cclorado Springs: David Cook Distribution.

Willmington, Dr. Harold L. 2011. *Willmington's Guide to the Bible*. Carol Stream, Illinois: Tyndale House Publishers.

About the Author

CORYNNE DAMM hails from the beautiful state of Virginia. Having grown up in a family where both parents served in the military, she was privileged to travel the world from a young age. She relishes reading, exploring picturesque locations, and writing historical fiction. As a full-time educator, she fulfills her greatest passion of teaching children. Finishing her master's degree in Christian education challenged her to consider the true Master Teacher—Jesus Christ.

Endnotes

1. Kent, Jr., "A Time to Teach," 9.
2. Walvoord and Zuck, *The Bible Knowledge Commentary: New Testament*, 124.
3. Sewall, "The Social Ethics of Jesus," 286.
4. Reddin, "Jesus the Rabbi," 697.
5. Walvoord and Zuck, *New Testament*, 272.
6. Walvoord and Zuck, *The Bible Knowledge Commentary: Old Testament*, 138.
7. Henry, *Matthew Henry's Concise Commentary*, 699.
8. Pentecost, *The Words and Works of Jesus Christ*, 132–135.
9. Walvoord and Zuck, *New Testament*, 285.
10. Cate, "Christ as Teacher," 24.
11. Walvoord and Zuck, *New Testament*, 224.
12. Walvoord and Zuck, *New Testament*, 226.
13. Wilmington, *Willmington's Guide to the Bible*, 237.
14. Henry, *Concise Commentary*, 743.

[15] Walvoord and Zuck, *New Testament*, 217.

[16] Walvoord and Zuck, *New Testament*, 321.

[17] Sewall, "The Social Ethics of Jesus," 272.

[18] Henry, *Matthew Henry's Concise Commentary*, 724.

[19] Walvoord and Zuck, *The Bible Knowledge Commentary: New Testament*, 215.

[20] Walvoord and Zuck, *New Testament*, 72.

[21] Ryrie, *Basic Theology*, 245.

[22] Pentecost, *The Words and Works of Jesus Christ*, 121.

[23] Cate, "Christ as Teacher," 26.

[24] Wiersbe, *Wiersbe's Expository Outlines on the New Testament*, 252.

[25] Henry, *Concise Commentary*, 955.

[26] Pettegrew, "Teaching Methods of Christ," 17.

[27] Willmington, *Willmington's Guide to the Bible*, 240.

[28] Sewall, "The Social Ethics of Jesus," 276.

[29] Willmington, *Willmington's Guide to the Bible*, 230.

[30] Henry, *Matthew Henry's Concise Commentary*, 757.

[31] Walvoord and Zuck, *The Bible Knowledge Commentary: New Testament*, 38.

32. Henry, *Concise Commentary*, 688.
33. Wiersbe, *Wiersbe's Expository Outlines on the New Testament*, 40.
34. Pentecost, *The Words and Works of Jesus Christ*, 537.
35. Sewall, 288.
36. Sewall, 277.
37. Reddin, "Jesus the Rabbi," 703.
38. Ryrie, *Basic Theology*, 323.
39. Hendricks, *Teaching to Change Lives*, 39.
40. Marzano, Pickering, and Pollock, *Classroom Instruction that Works*, 74.
41. Marzano, Pickering, and Pollock, *Classroom Instruction*, 75.
42. Pettegrew, "Teaching Principles of Christ," 5.
43. Braley, Layman, and White, *Foundations of Christian School Education*, 171.
44. Hendricks, 54.
45. Marzano, Pickering, and Pollock, *Classroom Instruction*, 104.
46. Pettegrew, "Teaching Principles," 13.
47. Marzano, Pickering, and Pollock, *Classroom Instruction*, 15.
48. Cate, "Christ as Teacher," 26.

[49] Kistemaker, "Jesus As Story Teller: Literary Perspectives On The Parables," 49.

[50] Anthony, *Christian Education: Foundations for the Twenty-first Century*, 114.

[51] Pettegrew, "Teaching Principles," 26.

[52] Martin, "Christ in the Classroom," 1.

[53] Braley, Layman, and White, 179.

[54] Hendricks, 38.

[55] Hendricks, 68.

[56] Hendricks, *Teaching to Change Lives*, 39.

[57] Kent, Jr., "A Time to Teach," 10.

[58] Hendricks, 74.

[59] Henry, *Matthew Henry's Concise Commentary*, 893.

[60] Walvoord and Zuck, *The Bible Knowledge Commentary: New Testament*, 28.

[61] Hendricks, 74.

[62] Walvoord and Zuck, *New Testament*, 28.

[63] Walvoord and Zuck, *New Testament*, 83-84.

[64] Wiersbe, *Wiersbe's Expository Outlines on the New Testament*, 241.

[65] Henry, *Concise Commentary*, 920.

[66] Ryrie *Basic Theology*, 457.

[67] Kent, Jr., 9.

[68] Hendricks, 74.

[69] Henry, *Concise Commentary*, 919–920.

[70] Willmington, *Willmington's Guide to the Bible*, 839.

[71] Hendricks, 73.

[72] Henry, *Concise Commentary*, 920.